HOW

MW00915942

TIPS AND TRICKS TO MAKE THE
PERFECT PIE CRUST EVERY TIME

Gladys Wealth

Contents

INTRODUCTION

This Homemade Pie Crust Recipe is buttery, flaky and it's my favourite. This guide will show you all the ideas and tricks on how easy it is to form pie crust from the scratch.

You can use this pie crust recipe for all types of delicious pies.

Making Homemade pie crust isn't as hard as I would think it is. In fact it is downright EASY if you've got the proper pie crust recipe.

CHAPTER ONE

My Buttery, Flaky Pie Crust Recipe

I won't pretend there's just one way to do that. There are many variations on fats, liquids, techniques which will all work! But after a couple of solid years of testing different recipes and methods, this all butter crust recipe is the one that I stand by. Not only is it easy, it tastes delicious.

Prep Time: 10 minutes

Category: Pie

Method: Oven

Ingredients:

- 2 1/2 cups all purpose flour

- 1 tablespoon of granulated sugar

- 1 teaspoon of salt

- 1 cup cold butter, cubed

- 2 teaspoons apple cider vinegar

- 1/2 cup ice water

Instructions

1. Combine the dry ingredients and the butter. In a large metal bowl, combine the flour, sugar, and salt. Add the cold cubed butter to the flour mixture and combine with a pastry cutter until the mixture resembles very coarse sand. This is perfectly fine if you have some larger pieces of butter on hand.

2. Stir in the vinegar and ice water with a wooden spoon until the dough becomes too difficult to knead; at that point, use your hands quickly to knead the dough until it holds together. If the dough is too dry or crumbles apart, add 1 tablespoon more water at a time until it holds together.

3. Cut the dough in half and shape each half into a flat circle. Wrap each dough in plastic wrap and place in the refrigerator for at least an hour and up to 3 days.

4. Roll out the dough. If using a standard 9-inch pie plate, roll the dough out 1/8 – 1/4-inch thick into a 12-inch circle on a lightly floured surface with a rolling pin when ready to use.

5. Fold or quarter the dough and place it carefully in a pie plate. Trim the edges of the crust, leaving about 1 inch overhanging, and press it lightly into the dish. Using your fingers, crimp the crust's edges.

6. Fill your pie with the desired filling.

7. If the recipe calls for it, roll out the remaining dough to make a top crust. Place the pie dough on top and crimp the edges to seal. Bake according to the directions on the pie recipe you're using. A fruit pie should be baked at 375°F for 45-50 minutes.

Is butter or shortening better for pie crust?

After some research and testing, I discovered that the other most popular preferred method is a combination of butter and shortening. And, to be honest, they both work fantastically well.

Here are some of the reasons why I prefer butter in pie crusts:

• **Butter simply tastes better!** I can always tell when a crust is made with shortening because it has that oily mouth-feel, which I don't like. Shortening is 100 percent fat, whereas butter is 80-85 percent fat.

• **Butter is used to make flaky pie crusts.** What is the other 20% of butter's fat if it's made up of 80% fat? Well, butter is about 15-20% water, and as that water evaporates as it bakes, it turns to steam, which puffs up the layers in the dough and creates a flaky crust! Science, man!

• **But use cold butter.** Because of its lower melting point, butter is a little more difficult to work with, so the main trick here is to keep it COLD. To create those tender flakes, you want little flecks of butter throughout the dough, and keeping the butter as cold as possible will help with that, which leads me to the next point...

CHAPTER TWO

Tips for making this simple pie crust

Perfect Pie Crust Tip No. 1: Keep Everything COLD!!

Not only should the butter be cold, but so should the water you use, in fact, ICE WATER is the best! I measure out the water for the recipe and add a few ice cubes to make it as cold as possible.

If you want, you can even chill your bowl!

If you live in a warm climate, you can even use frozen butter. This is a great trick that works perfectly because if you're making an all butter pie crust in a humid or warm environment, the butter can soften up pretty quickly, so place it in the freezer 30-ish minutes before you're going to make your crust.

Perfect Pie Crust Tip No. 2: Cube Your Butter!

This is a critical step! Before or after cubing, the butter can be chilled... OR EVEN BOTH! Cubing the butter before adding it to the flour mixture expedites the entire process, which is exactly what you want. It is critical that you make your dough as quickly as possible! Remember that you want little pockets of butter throughout the dough, and if the butter is warm, it will all melt together.

Consider it this way... Put a whole stick of butter in a bowl and get out your pastry cutter... How much longer will it take you to mash an entire stick of butter into small pieces versus if the butter was already cubed? Doesn't that make sense?

What Flour Should You Use For Pie Crust?

I recommend using a good all-purpose flour. I prefer Bob's Red Mill Unbleached All Purpose Flour, but you can use whatever all-purpose flour you have on hand and it will still be okay.

You may be wondering why pastry flour is not preferred when making pie dough. A pie crust is a type of pastry. Pie crust made with pastry flour is undeniably delicious and tender, as pastry flour contains less protein than all-purpose flour, but it does not hold up as well as all-purpose flour crust. If you want a flaky, yet sturdy crust for your pie, I highly recommend all-purpose flour.

How to Roll Out and Decorate a Pie Crust

Rolling out a pie crust is a simple process. Here are a few pointers for making a pie crust that won't fall apart when you roll it out:

1.   **Allow at least an hour for your dough to chill before rolling it out.** This is a step I always recommend because it allows the gluten in the flour to relax before stretching it out further. My goal is always a flaky crust, and this step definitely helps!

2.   **Lightly flour your work surface and keep a few tablespoons of flour on hand for when you need it!** To prevent sticking on the top, lightly flour both the rolling pin and the rolling surface as you roll out your dough! Nothing is more frustrating than having everything perfectly rolled out only to have it stick to the counter!

3.   **3. Roll your dough to a thickness of 1/8 – 1/4 inch.** It doesn't have to be exact, but I've made the mistake of rolling my crust too thin, which doesn't make for a very stable base for your pie. But make sure it's not too thick, because you want it to bake all the way through. This recipe yields enough dough for two circles of dough.

4.   In addition to the thickness of the dough, roll it out to be 2-inches wider in diameter than a standard pie plate, or 4-inches wider if using a deep dish pie plate. Make sure there is enough excess hanging over the edge to allow you to crimp the crust's edge!

5.   To transfer the dough from the rolling surface to the plate, fold it into halves or quarters before placing it in the pan. If you're a pie pro, you can roll it around the rolling pin and use that technique, but I never seem to be able to do so!

6.   DO NOT BE WORRIED if your pie dough cracks or tears!! Simply wet your fingers with water and mold it back together.

7.   Once your pie dough is in the pan, use a pairing knife to trim the edges, leaving about an inch overhanging. If you want to make dough decorations like leaves or stars, save some extra dough.

Can Pie Crust Dough Be Freezed?

Certainly! Freezing dough is a great way to prepare ahead of time. You can either freeze the dough in a ball or press it into a pie plate. If you've blind baked a crust and intend to fill it later, you can even freeze it already baked.

More Pie Crust Tips & Tricks to Make the Perfect Pie Crust Every Time

1. Do not grease the pie plate. There's enough fat in the dough that you shouldn't have any problems with sticking!

2. In my pie crust, I like to use 2 teaspoons of vinegar. What is the purpose of putting vinegar in pie crust? Because the vinegar aids in the prevention of gluten formation, a tender crust is produced.

3. Don't be concerned about the crust's appearance. For a long time, this was a major source of frustration for me. It would keep me from even making pies because they were always so sloppy! BUT...the here's thing...pie is supposed to be rustic. It's all right. Unless you're entering a pie contest, how it looks isn't that important.

Purchase a Pastry Cutter as well (Pastry Blender)

This is one of those vexing kitchen tools that gets stuck in your drawer and takes up valuable space. I understand how inconvenient it is. It's simply the simplest tool for cutting butter into pie dough. They're inexpensive, so it's not a big investment, and I'll tell you, they're useful for more than just pie crust! It's great for making guacamole!

BUT, if you don't have a pastry cutter and don't intend to buy one, here are a few alternatives:

• **A fork:** It will take a little longer, and the tines are closer together than a pastry blender, but it will do the job.

• **A food processor:** Many people I know swear by a food processor when it comes to making pie dough. It's actually a great idea because you can pulse it until it's done and you won't overwork your ingredients. I'm just lazy and despise having to dig out my food processor!

• **Knives for butter:** Two butter knives can also be used; it's just a little more difficult!

• **A grater for cheese.** If you plan to freeze your butter, I recommend using a cheese grater. Otherwise, it becomes mushy!

• **Your Hands.** This is a last resort because the heat from your hands quickly warms the butter. So, if this is what you intend to do, freeze your butter!

If you're making a pie with a no-bake filling, you'll want to pre-bake your crust, also known as "blind baking." Let's go over how simple this is...

1. You will complete all of the steps in the recipe exactly as written.

2. Fit one of the rolled-out dough circles into a pie plate, pinching the edges together to form a crust. Poke holes in the bottom of the crust with a fork to help prevent bubbles. Freeze the pie crust for at least

30 minutes. This will keep your crust from shrinking while baking.

3. Preheat the oven to 375 degrees Fahrenheit (375°F).

4. Cut a circle of parchment paper the size of your rolled crust and place it inside the frozen crust. Pie weights or dried beans can be placed on top of the parchment paper. As you bake the pie, this mimics the filling, holding it in place and preventing bubbles in the crust, as well as the pricked holes you made with the fork.

5. Bake the crust for 15 minutes. Remove the crust from the oven and peel away the parchment paper and weights. Return the crust to the oven for an additional 10- 15 minutes, or until golden. If the crust begins to brown too quickly, cover it with a pie crust shield or aluminum foil and continue baking.

What exactly is a Pie Shield?

A pie shield will be your best friend if you plan on baking pies. I went years without one, scraping aluminum foil together to make a makeshift shield to keep my pie crust from browning too much.

However, the handy pie shield invention is a SUPER simple tool for ensuring that your crust does not become too brown. They're inexpensive and, in my opinion, well worth it!

Made in the USA
Coppell, TX
23 July 2024

35080924R00016